About

Seven Etudes & Reflections is a collection of piano pieces composed over the past year, serving as a sequel to my previous piano book, *Tides and Other Works for Piano*. This new book features shorter pieces with more simplified musical forms, and compositions that are more accessible to interpret—designed for friends and students to exercise their skills while having fun.

The first part of the book, *Seven Etudes*, consists of the pieces featured on my album *Seven Etudes for Piano*. These new works share a similar approach to my earlier piano compositions, both in style and pianism—original music with hints of Latin American folk, jazz, and contemporary classical music, crafted to gracefully balance technical challenge and singable melodies.

In the second part of the book, *Seven Reflections*, each Etude is mirrored by its corresponding Reflection. The term 'reflection' can take on various meanings—it may share the same tonality, a similar initial motif, a comparable groove, or simply the idea of composing with a specific Etude in mind. Additionally, I aimed for the Reflections to be easier to play than the Etudes.

Both sections of the book share a common characteristic: the music is highly 'pianistic.' It 'fits well' in the hand, is easy to read and memorize, and incorporates various 'pianistic tricks' that allow us to sound virtuosic while performing something deceptively simple. A common theme also emerges through these pieces: a sense of simplicity, intimacy, and a minimalistic approach to musical and pianistic elements.

Notes

The use of the pedal is left to each pianist's discretion. Pedal markings are only included in sections where it is essential for a specific effect or where the pedal is used in an unconventional way.

Several pieces in this collection include optional sections for improvisation. Each piece is effective with or without these sections, leaving the choice entirely up to the interpreter. It is worth noting that the vocabulary for these improvisations is not rooted in jazz or any specific style; for this reason, I have chosen not to include chord symbols, allowing the performer complete freedom. My hope is that each musician feels comfortable and confident enough to expand on the written material, bringing their own creativity and ideas into play.

The material in this book is organized into two separate sections: one for *Etudes* and another for *Reflections*. However, the interpreter is encouraged to experiment with different sequences and combinations of these pieces, whether in practice or performance. For example, playing *Etude #1* followed by *Reflection #1* allows the mirroring effect to be more clearly heard.

I hope you enjoy this book as much as I enjoyed composing these pieces.

Emilio Teubal, 2025

Etudes		Reflections	
8	#1	48	#1
11	#2	50	#2
18	#3	53	#3
22	#4	58	#4
27	#5	61	#5
35	#6	65	#6
38	#7	68	#7

Published by Emilio Teubal (BMI)

Copyright © 2025 by Emilio Teubal
All rights reserved.

No part of this publication may be reproduced, stored in retrieval system, or transmitted, in any form or by any means (electronic, mechanical, photocopying, recording or otherwise) without the prior written permission.

Artwork and design by Alex Rearick
Music Engraving by Felipe Traine

emilioteubal.com

Etudes

Etude 1

Emilio Teubal

Etude 2

Emilio Teubal

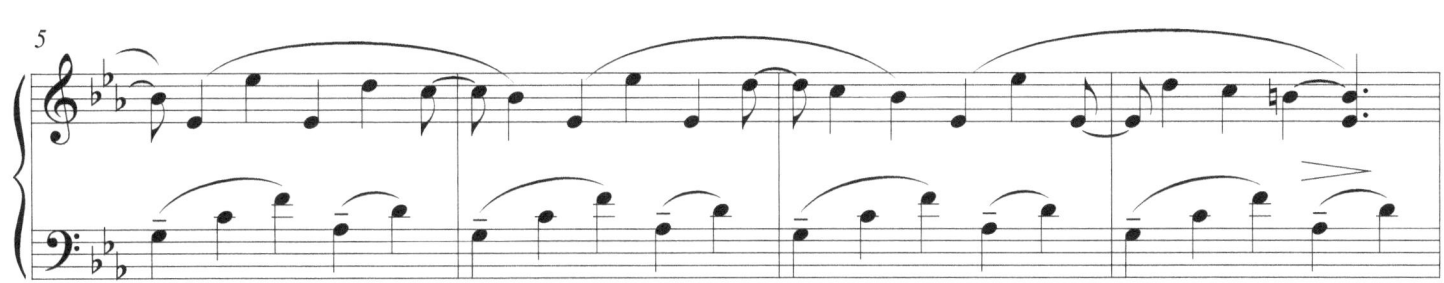

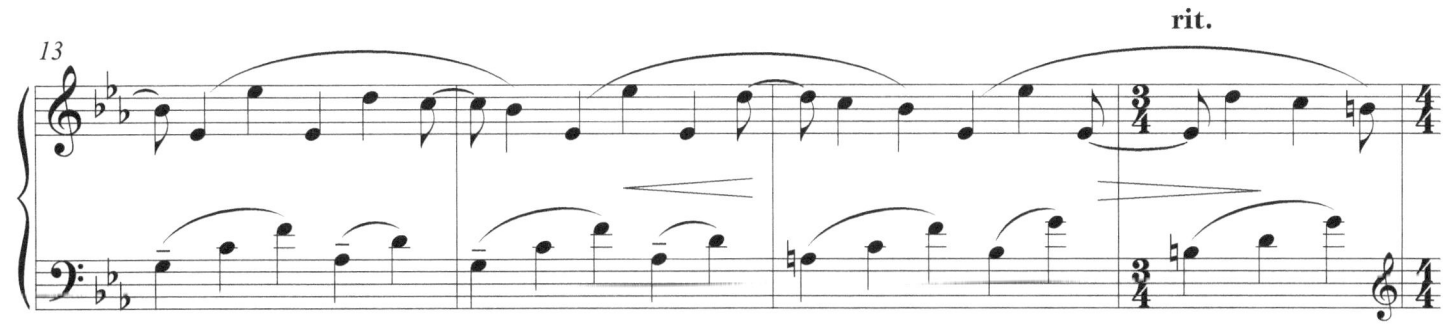

Copyright ©2025 Emilio Teubal (BMI)
All Rights Reserved

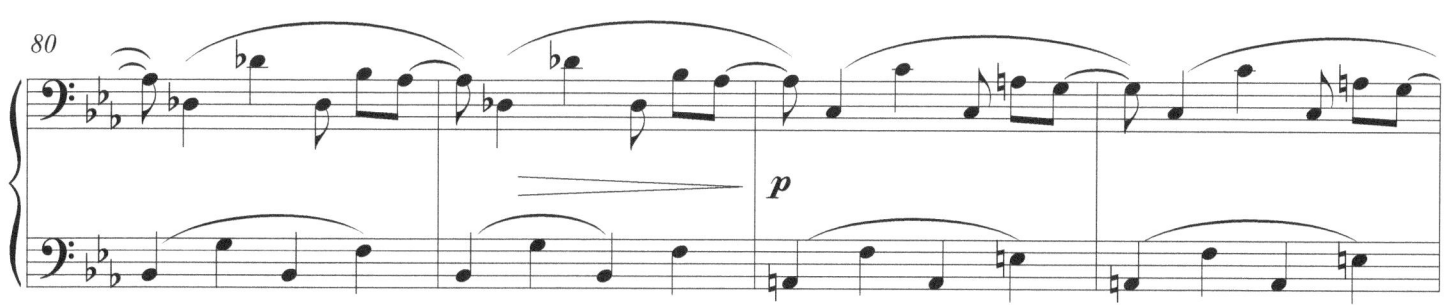

16 Etude 2

(𝅗𝅥.) only on repeat

Etude 3

Emilio Teubal

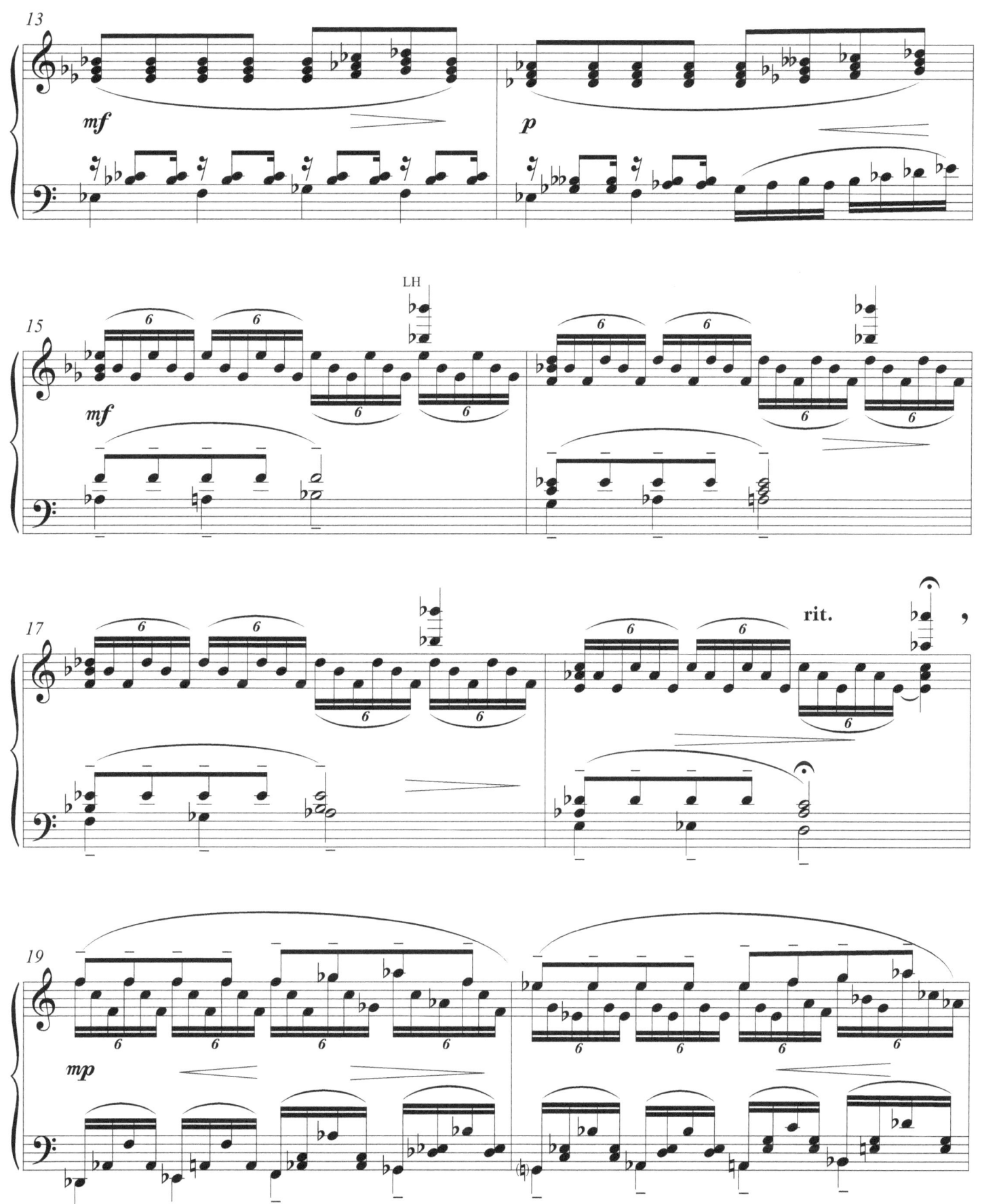

20 Etude 3

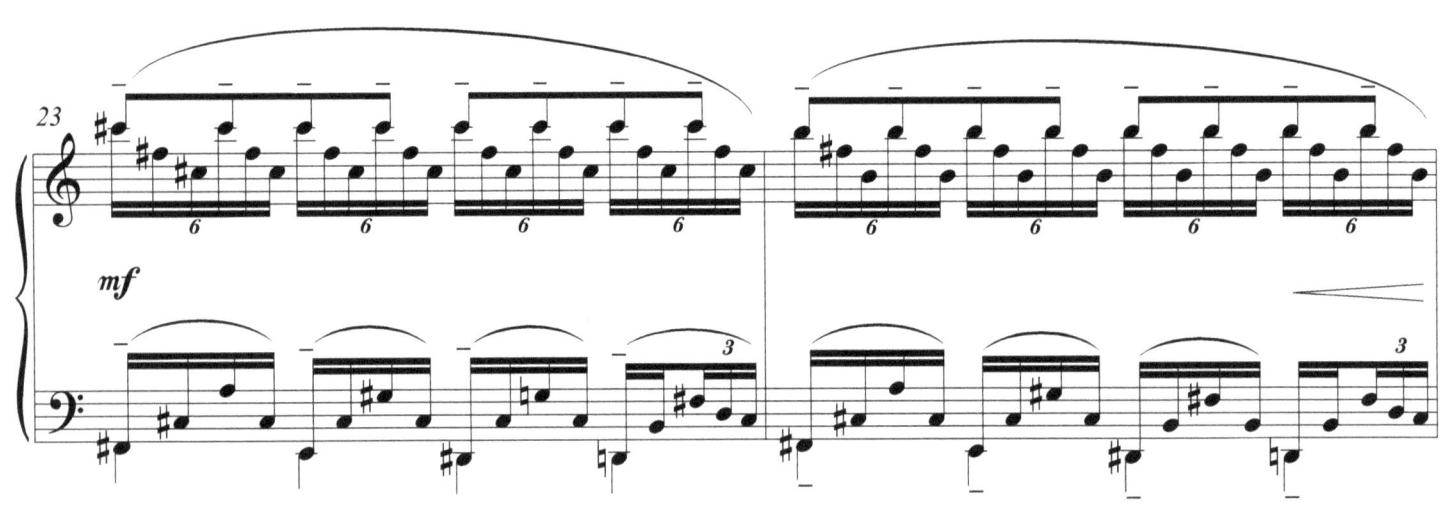

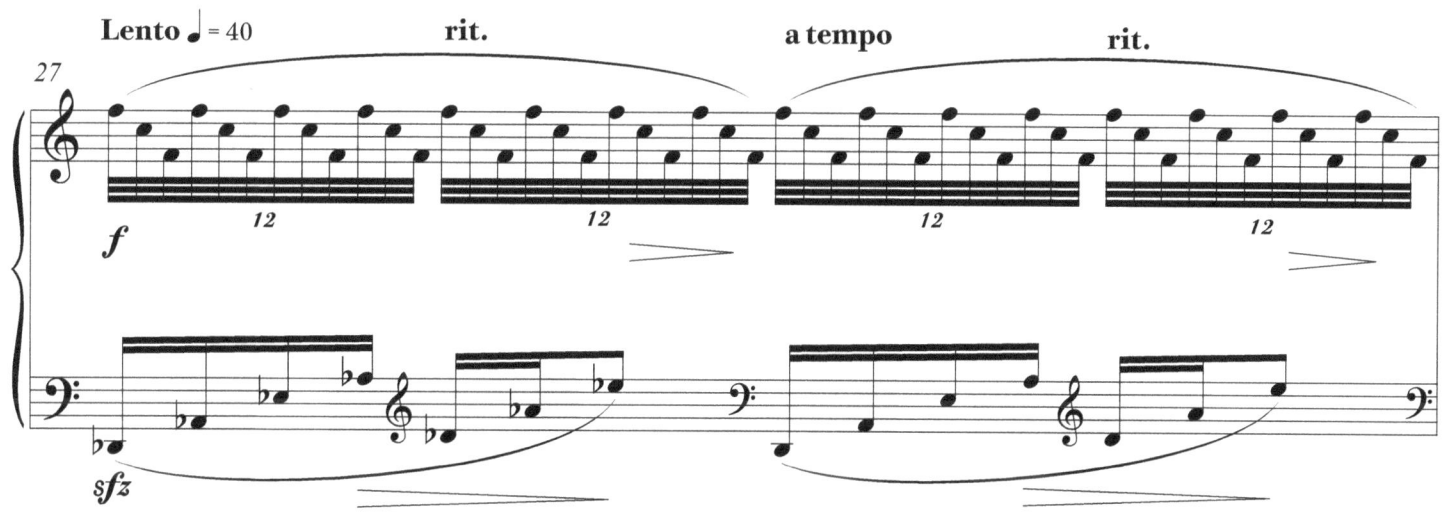
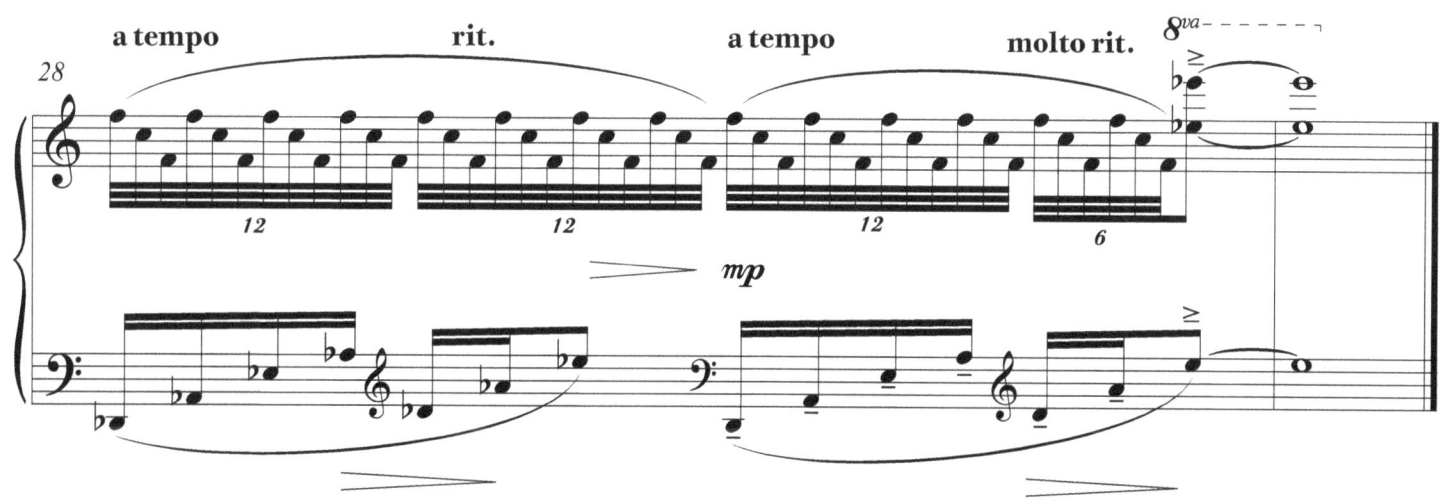

Etude 4

alla Brad

Emilio Teubal

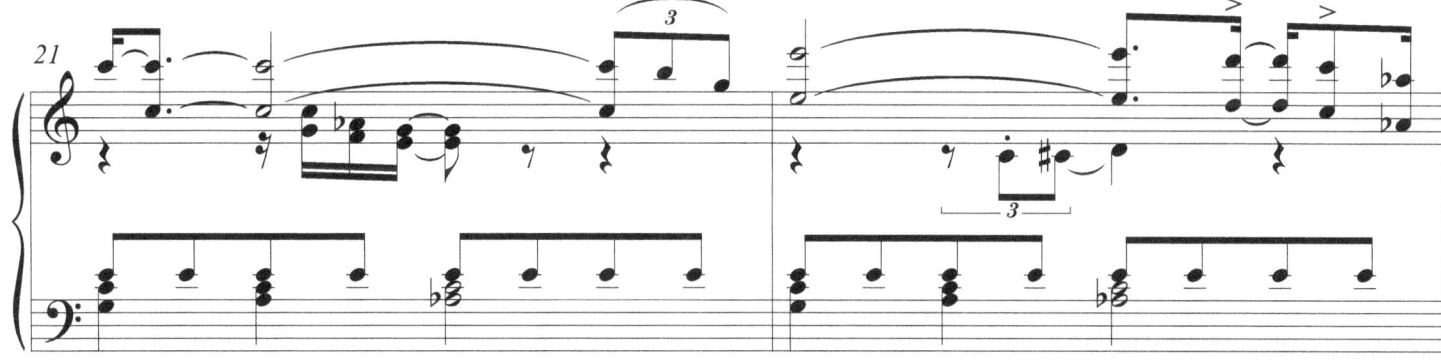

Etude 5

Emilio Teubal

28

Etude 5

Etude 6

Aires de Vidala

Emilio Teubal

Etude 6

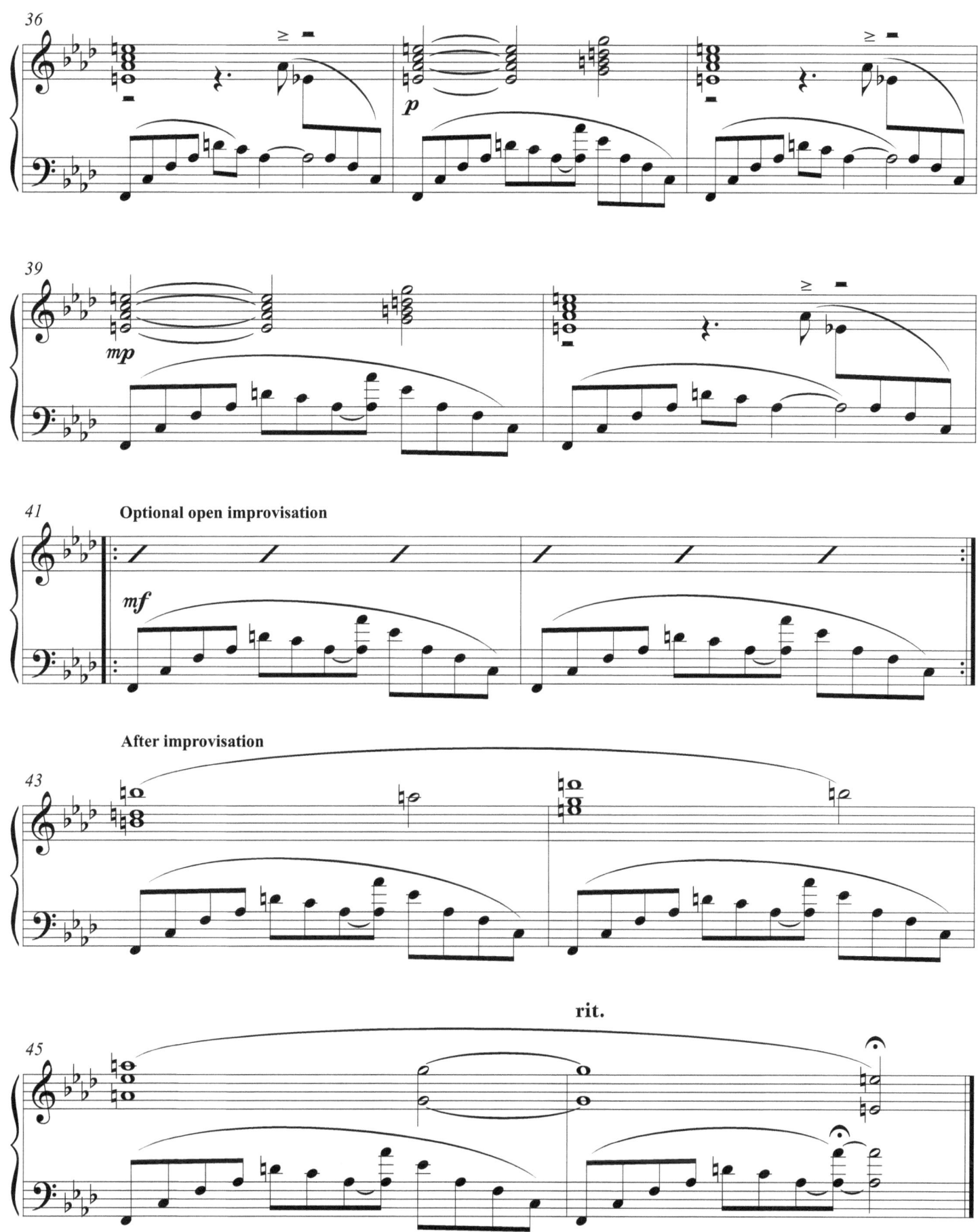

Etude 7

Extremos / Rupture

Emilio Teubal

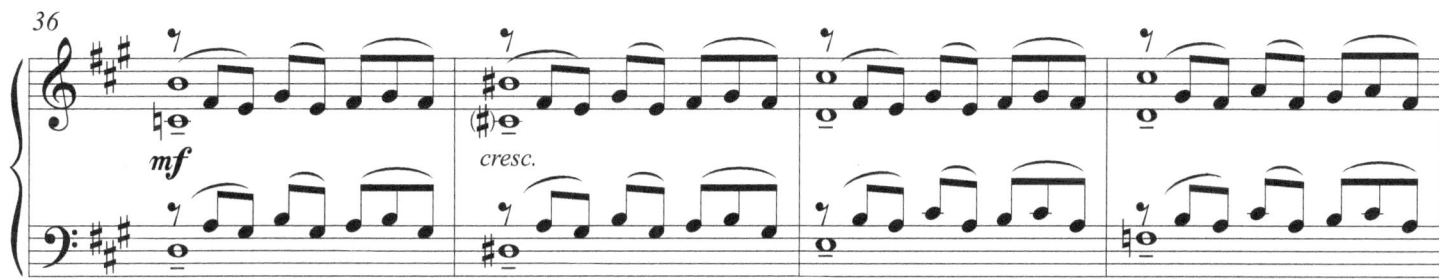

Etude 7

Reflections

Reflection 1

Emilio Teubal

Reflection 2

Aires de Maracatu

Emilio Teubal

Reflection 3

Reflejo de un Huayno

Emilio Teubal

Copyright ©2025 Emilio Teubal (BMI)
All Rights Reserved

Reflection 4

Emilio Teubal

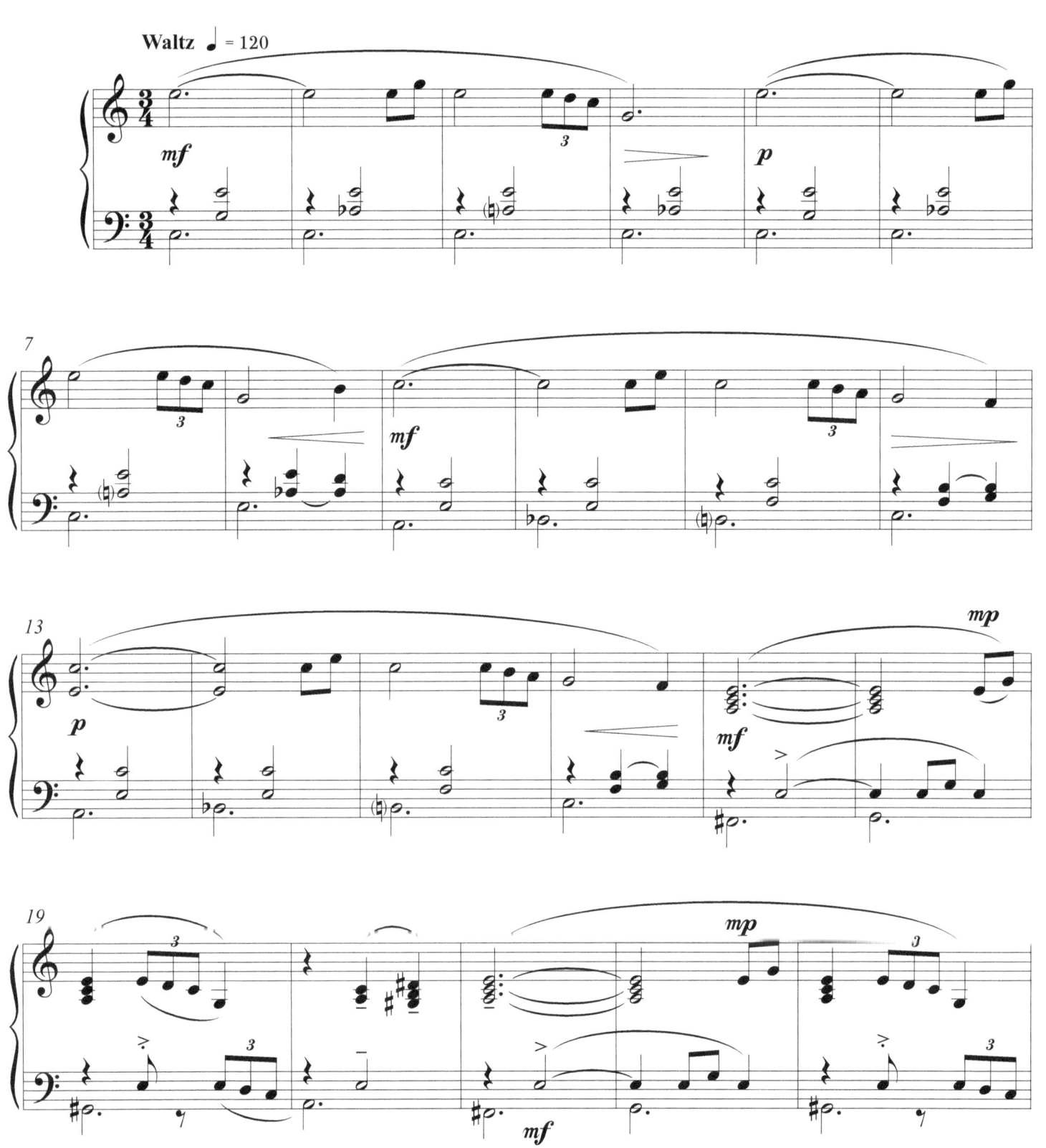

Copyright ©2025 Emilio Teubal (BMI)
All Rights Reserved

Reflection 5

Emilio Teubal

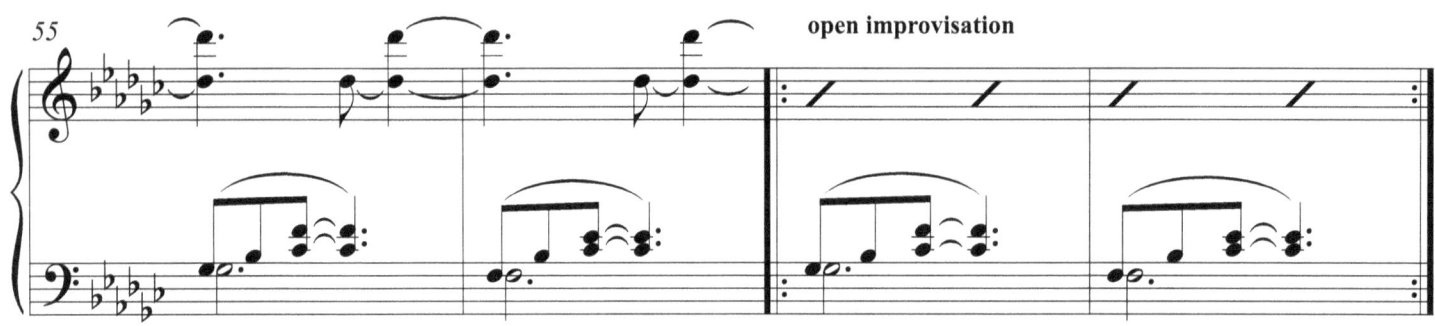

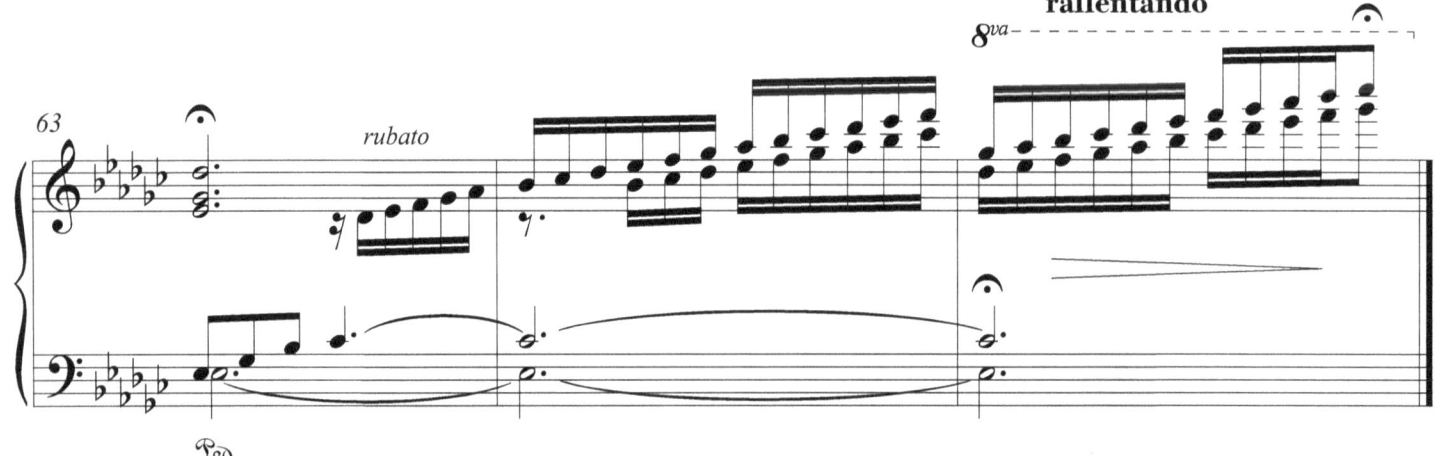

Reflection 6

Emilio Teubal

Lento ♩ = 70

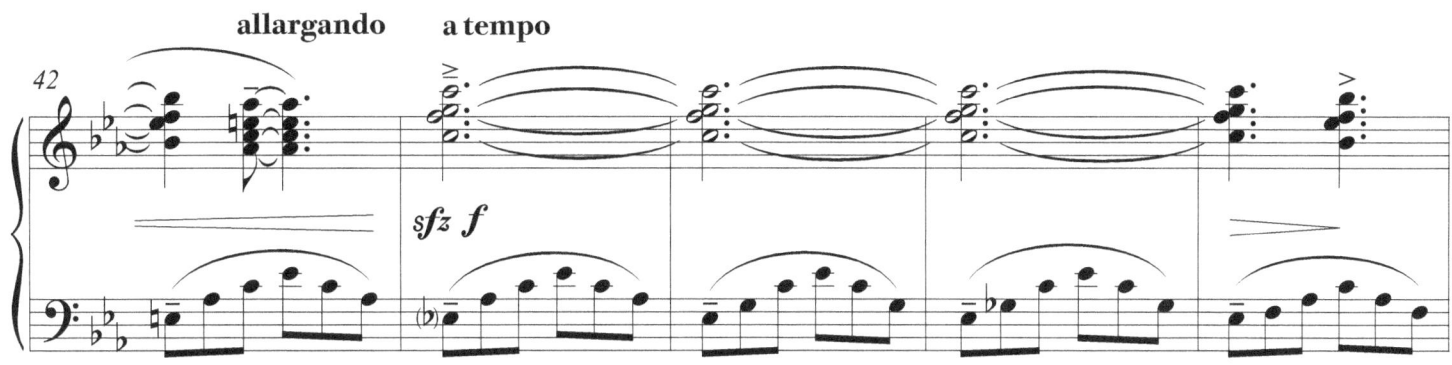
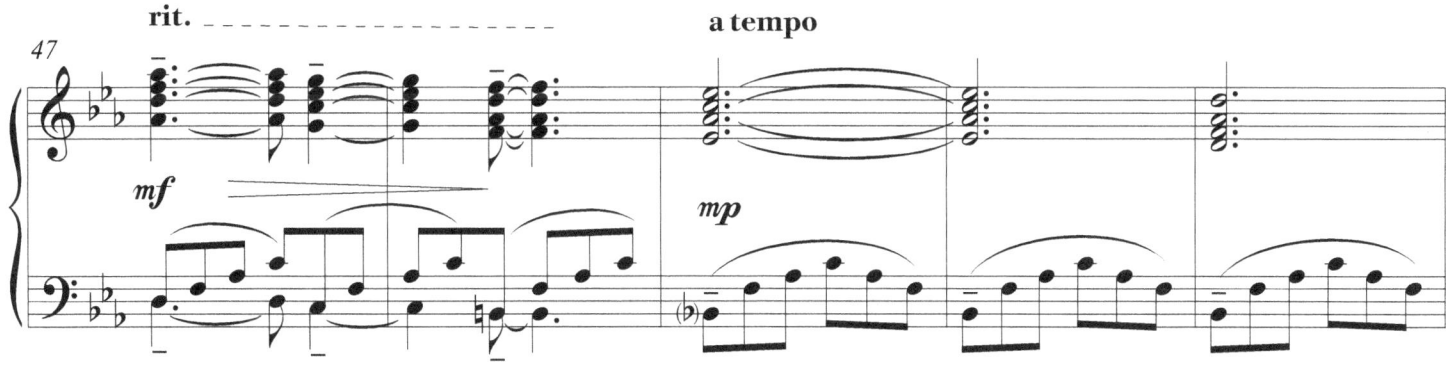
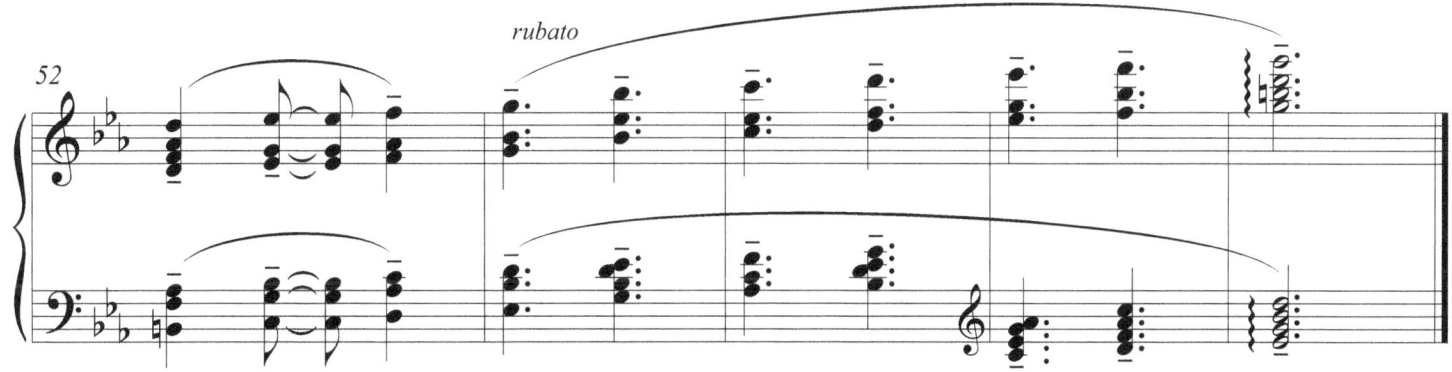

Reflection 7

Emilio Teubal

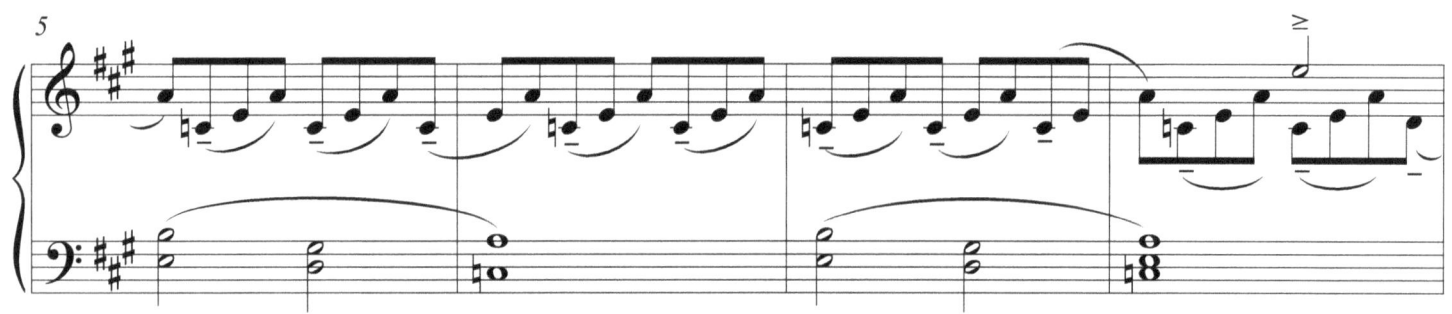

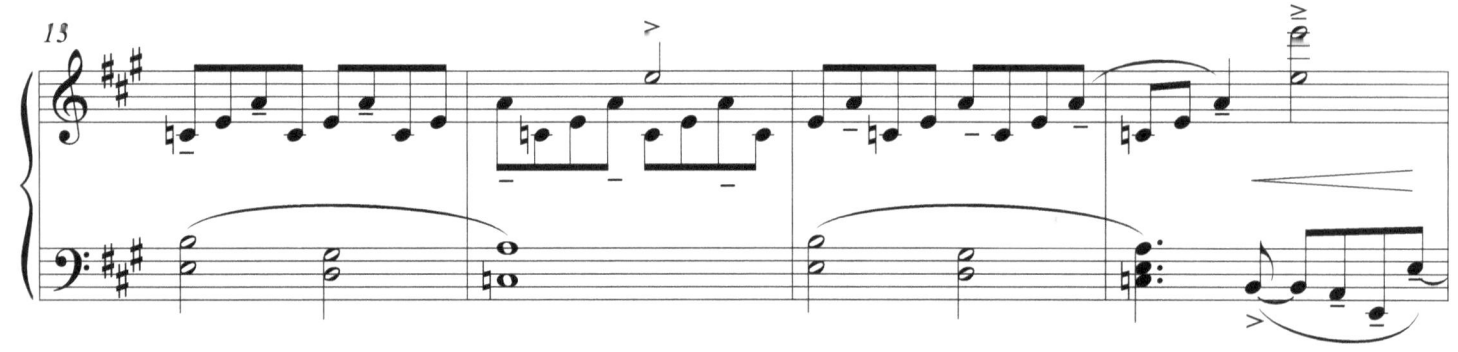

Copyright ©2025 Emilio Teubal (BMI)
All Rights Reserved

Thanks

Alex Rearick, Felipe Traine, Diyora Tursunova,
Theresa Rosas, Chris Michael, Carlos Fagin,
Pablo Lepegna, and Tupac Teubal.

www.ingramcontent.com/pod-product-compliance
Lightning Source LLC
Chambersburg PA
CBHW080349170426
43194CB00014B/2737